ANTHEMS FROM A BLACK WOMEN

JO EVANS LYNN

FOUNDATION, Publishers, Greensboro, NC 27406

Copyright 2021 Jo Evans Lynn

No part of this book may be copied or reproduced in any form without the written consent of the author or her heirs.

This1Matters Foundation, Greensboro, NC

ISBN: 978-1-7369837-2-0

Dedication

To my sisters in faith and blood, you have all enriched my life with love.

The Black Woman's Anthem

I am Hausa, Fulani, Galla, Dinka,
Yoruba, Masai, Ibo, Ashanti
And more…

I am helpmate, sister, mother,
Daughter, lover, niece, friend,
All this and more…

I have worked beside men in the fields
Just as hard and just as long.
I have raised children that
Weren't even my own.

I have stood by my man when
There wasn't another soul
To help him through
I am comfort, love, tenderness, strength,
And a resting place.

I am the princess of the Nile,
A Nubian queen
An ebony empress,
I am
A Black Woman.

Changelings

Three things remain.
Undaunted.
Unchanged.
Through slavery
And Jim Crow
Though the fear, pain,
Hatred, and violence
Could have lynched them right out
Of us,
But it didn't.
They couldn't.
For we knew then
What we still know.
All that we were -Nubian princesses
and kings,
All that we are - Changelings in a
changing land,
All that we will be -Still here and
finally free,
Is in us
And ever will be.

The Mountain High

The majesty and strength of Kilimanjaro
Nestles within a package
Well under six feet tall
The courage to come through
Every pain and hardship
Bound in corsets.
Tightly girdled, but there
Waiting to be set free.
Love and caring are shouted
On gentle whispers and caresses.
Restoring hope and faith
A flood of loyalty
Gushes forth to a child, a man, or a friend.

All this flows from
The mountain stream that is
WOMAN.

A Love Psalm

My father, My God
My good and faithful lover
In You alone can I discover
All I was meant to be
No words from my mouth are worthy
Of all that you are to me.
Giver of life I adore thee
Steel bridge over valley and dale
Against Thee every other lover pales.

I call you and you answer
I need you and you are there.
You are my brick house
And strong shelter
You break every fetter.

The skyscrapers of my life
Are like Philistines,
Against Your might
You are water in the
Barren desert of my life.
And my bulwark against every form of strife.
You are the Love of my life.

Casting Stones

Harlots, sluts,
Whores, crumpets, and freaks
Nasty names for women
Who do nasty things.
But men are called
Rascals, Players, and such.
Those names are somewhat mild-
Call a man a Player and most times
he'll smile.

I'm glad the Bible has no mixed
protocol
Two terms fit all.
Sinners while we're in it,
And Saved when we repent.

My Sisters

You are my sisters!
We are bound to one another
By our faith
Hope in Jesus Christ
and all that He put in us.

My Sisters,
Do you know how remarkable?
Our legacy is?
We are heirs of the strength of Queen
Candance
Whose army of warriors riding elephants
Forced Alexander the Great to retreat to
Egypt.

We inherited a beauty that
Other races use surgery and globs of
makeup
Trying to imitate
Our juicy lips,
Rich chocolate skin and soulful brown
eyes
Lord knows we should wear them with a
great deal of pride!

We are Sisters.

Our legacy of faith goes all the way back
to
Joanna, Priscilla, and Aquila
Sisters who used
Their personal resources
To support the ministry
Of Jesus
And explained the way of God
To new Christians.

We are Sisters and
Because of the tears, laughter, and
prayers
That bind us
We stand together under
The veil of God's grace.
Knowing that as sisters we must love
And support one another
Like our mothers and aunts did back in
olden days

LouBelle, Syretha, Goldie, do you
remember
That black lace dress and hat
That was passed around from Sister to
Sister
January to December
Until it became the Official Funeral
Outfit

Of the Women of Wells?

We are sister solders in the army of the Lord.
The Jehovah Witnesses didn't have anything
On the women of Wells
When it came to going out among the people
Talking about the love of Jesus
And gleaning
Money to support the radio ministry.

You are my sisters!
I kneel with you in prayer
Steadfast in
the hope of Glory
Which is our main strategy
As women of faith
Because the mystery that is
Christ in us is revealed
When we pray and stand together.

You Don't Know

You don't know what's under this here
hat.
Whether knaps or curls
This here hat is on a lady's head.
A lady who's not stuck up
I'm looking up.

There was a time when my hair got
sweat back
And I didn't make nary a dime.
The master thought this body was his
stead of mine.
But under this here hat on a Sunday
morning
I was a lady.

Child, you don't know what's under this
here hat.
I been spit at and told to get in my place
At the back of the bus or at the take-out-
counter,
On the back of the bus!
While I was on my way
To clean their houses
And care for their children,
But under this here hat, there was front
of the bus pride

And the best education the Colored
schools could provide.

Some Sundays didn't nobody but me
and the Lord know
What was knapped up in time to go to
the beauty salon.
Miss Sadie said she forgot to come on
home.
Said she and the other ladies were too
busy sipping their mint juleps at the
Country Club.
Made me so late, I had to walk home
from downtown
And cook Sunday dinner.
But under this here hat on Sunday
morning, I looked up steada down
I sang, "Yes Lord"
Steada, "Yes Ma'am."

Under this here hat I was serving the
only one who'd paid a cost
High enough to own my soul.

So, don't say cause I'm wearing my hats
That I'm high and mighty and thinking
too much of myself.
I've earned the right to this hear hat.
Cause it was me and women like me

Who bore the backhands, lashes, and
verbal slights
So, you can go without a hat today
And still be called a lady.

Hope

The worst thing about hope
Is when it's gone you feel
A whole lot worse off.

The best thing about hope
Is having just enough
To keep you holding on
Until…

We Were Blessed

(Tribute to Dorothy Lynn McNabb)

God blessed us with Dot.
For she loved us.
She cared for everyone
For as long as she could…
Her generosity was overwhelming.
She gave all she could
For as long as she could…
She taught us how to be a family.

She held us close
For as long as she could
No link was too distant
For her to claim
First, second, third cousin
Born in or married in,
Lived near or far
Or in the house on Olivia Lane

She knew every name.
If you lost touch
With a family member,
All you had to do was call Dorothy
If she didn't have their number,
She wouldn't stop until she
Found someone who did.

Every family needs a Dorothy.
That one family member who glues
All of the family together
With love and kindness.
We were blessed to have her,
For seldom has one family member
Touched so many lives
And left such a legacy of love.

Inside Out

When I found myself
Living inside a woman
That I didn't know
One that I would never have chosen to be
I knew it was time
To run for my life
To get away from the pain and the strife.
Time to turn myself inside out
Like the pockets of that coat
That I hadn't worn in years.
Lo and behold
I found pennies of strength
And a whole dollar worth of
Hope that I could be all that
God made me to be.

They Are Confused

They don't know what to do with
us.
They tell us we can't
Do this or that
Then they get mad
And start acting all bad.
When we show them that we can
Do all things through Christ that
strengthens us.
They say there is no way we're
Going there or doing that
Then it crushes their theories of
patriarchy
When we not only get there but do
that better
than they ever did it.
They watch us doing what they said
was impossible
And just shake their heads.
It's a shame that they have
something this special
And they just don't know what to
do
With us!

The Next Time He Calls...

Isn't God amazing?
Over the course of centuries
He created a
Trillion million women
And every single one of us
Has a higher calling stored inside
Each of us
If in him we abide.

It was there
This special calling on our lives
At the beginning.
It was reborn in the resurrection of the
Son
And if by chance, we don't pull it out
And put it to use
It will still be there at the end.
God never takes it back
No matter what kind of mess we are in.

And because He is God
I guess he just passes
It along to the next generation.

Who Knows?

Do you.
And I'll do me.
I'll be the best me
I can be.

And you?
Only you can decide
What you've got inside
Just make up your mind that God
Doesn't make mistakes
Nappy hair
Juicy lips
Bouncing booty
And all.
Just do you.

Still, I Stood

I grew up in a country where my people
Were forced to go to public bathrooms
That were cesspools- no tissue or water
to wash our hands.
Still, I stood.
The schools were segregated
The books had been used.
Only the teachers and principals were
any good.
Still, I stood.
Because the wages for Blacks were so
low,
I watched my father work two
sometimes three jobs.
Dying young- his heart worn out at the
age of 57.
Still, I stood.
I watched nearly every young man in the
Class of '67
Go to war when they were drafted.
Some not returning
Others returning broken.
I watched this happen while thousands
of white men

Ran to Canada or paid doctors
To credit them with draft dodging ailments.
Still, I stood.
I watched with horror as men who fought for our freedom-
Medgar Evers, Martin Luther King, John F. Kennedy, Robert Kennedy
All were shot by men who wanted my people to remain chained
To the racist rules of Jim Crow.
Still, I stood.
I watched with pride as young men risked their futures
By taking a knee,
To protest a murderous trend of killing unarmed Black Men
Still, I stood.
I watched a nation of Brown skinned Americans
Being treated like their lives had less value
than Americans in Texas and Florida.
Still, I stood.
I will no longer stand for a flag

Or for an anthem that is being used by
A heartless politician
To advance his racist agenda
By demanding football players be treated like high price slaves
Rather than like free men.
I will not stand as long as America's president is a man who
Dishonors the flag, the anthem, and the ideals
That these symbols
Must stand for in the home of the free
And the land of the brave.

Just Once

I'd done it
I'd finally gotten straight A's
Not one single grade below 95
It was the conduct grade
That had nearly pushed me to insanity
Holding back the hundred million questions
And comments that extended each lesson for me,
but the teacher called impertinent.
For that A in conduct, I'd bitten
My lips until they bled
Leaving all those questions and comments unsaid.
The morning after report card day
I was sure I'd
Get a comment written by my mother
That said something other than
"She can do better."
I was the first one downstairs
Even though I knew
We wouldn't get our signed report cards
Until we were marching out the door after breakfast.
When I looked down at my Report card
It said, "She Can do better."

"Mama! I cried, "I can't do better than
all A's"
"I didn't see any 100's." She calmly
replied.
"No. Ma'am but 95's and 98's are A's."
"Like I said you can do better.
Now, go on to school and do like I say."
I pouted about it all day.
But at the end of the year,
I got all 100's
The best I could do at the end of the
sixth grade.
But I knew my whole life through,
That I could always do better.

Pecking Order

God,
Husband,
Children,
Family
Friends,
Job,
Then self.

Sometimes we forget to squeeze ourselves in.
We tuck our feelings and needs out of sight.
Forgetting that if we don't love ourselves

We can't love anyone else right.

The Foundation of Prayer

We believe

In God

We believe He

Answers believing prayer.

We believe God is faithful

We believe God cares for us.

We believe He is our rock

We believe that He will open
Any door if we will just knock,

With prayers of faith.

We believe that our Prayers
will be answered

If only in Him we believe.

The Answer Is in You

When is enough

Enough?

Girl, only you can answer that.

You say, "This is the last tear I cry.

This is the last time I blame Me

Instead of them.

Is this the time

You say I'm through

And mean it?

Different but the Same

In God's Image
God created Man and Woman
In his image created he them.
Both strong , but in different ways
We may not be able to unscrew the lid
off that jar of mayonnaise
But we can carry a 40-pound child
1,225 miles
From starvation and violence
In Guatemala
To the Texas border.
Formed in the image
Of the one who created us.
Man and Woman
Tempered by the past
That has shaped us
Steeped in the faith
That saved us.
When we stand together
As One
No power on earth can take us apart.

The Pure Truth

Well now,
I'm gonna tell you exactly
How I feel.
I'm sick and tired
Of playing these racist games.
Don't grin in my face
And call me your friend
Then I find out you had a party
At your new house
And when I stopped by with a
House-warming gift
You didn't even invite me in.
I'm not gonna be your token
Colored friend anymore.
I'm slamming the door on your
Grinning face.

Once Upon a Time

I'm not sure what love feels like.
Is it that feeling that holds you
There year after year
Eyes starry with unshed tears?
Waiting for that fairy tale
Happily, ever after
That never comes
Or is it that
last little drop of hope…

Pathways

Our roads intersect

Walking in His Word

Our paths might wind and wind.

Twisting and turning

Especially when we get out of line,

But in the end, we must find

Ourselves in the same place

Walking on common ground

In a place where power

And love abounds

Trudging along on Holy Ground.

I'm just saying...

I cannot understand all this uproar about having to be in church to celebrate Easter. I guess it's the same people who claim that children can't pray in school because "They took prayer out of the schools" "They" meaning the government.

I know that was never true. Lord knows, I prayed my way through chemistry right there in the middle of Mrs. Gravely's class.

No one needs permission to pray anywhere if they have a relationship with God. Jesus taught us how to pray because He knew that there would be times when we needed Him and couldn't get to a church or a synagogue.

I love my church, Wells Memorial COGIC and I have been a member since 1957. Going to church, sharing corporate prayer and worship with my sisters and brothers in Christ is as much a part of me as my name.

But I can pray anywhere, I can connect with God in my home because the tomb was empty on Easter morning. People, it's all right if the churches are empty

Sunday morning. He is and ever will be wherever people lift their voices in prayer.

Unintentional Mess

I never meant
to give you
that kind of power over my life.

You were the kryptonite
to my not so super woman.

The strength of my love turned
Into a weakness
I spent years trying to overcome.
There were days when I didn't think I
could do it
That I couldn't break loose
But I did.
Thank God!

Liars Lie

They make up stuff and call it
A conspiracy theory.
Although they know it's a lie.

They say
Guns don't kill
People do.
Tell that to the mother
Whose son died from a gunshot wound
so big
They had to stuff his chest with saw
dust.

They say
Staying home to keep Covid-19
From spreading hurts the economy
Worse than trying to save lives.
Tell that to the wife who watched her
husband die at home
Fighting to breathe his last breath
Never being tested
Because politicians decided
That it was easier to lie
Than to prepare for the Pandemic
That the WHO warned on January 13
Had started to spread all over the world.
Admitting that the threat was real

Would hurt the president's election
chances.
So, they spent 70 days
Saying, "It's another Dem hoax
Don't pay any attention folks."
And Americans died.

They said, "It is nothing new
Just another flu."
While testing themselves and everyone
around them.
They said go out and protest staying in.
This darn flu is making people
Act like one nation under God again
And that just won't do
for the president's chances.
And in September
Americans died.
And God help us
They are still lying!

Us

I wonder

If mankind

Will ever learn to be kind

To one another.

When will race

Or place

Of birth

No matter where on earth

Place us in the same category?

God's children.

The 411

You want to know how I do it.

How I can laugh

When someone I thought would love me forever

Throws me away like a twice used tissue.

How I can smile when that bill

Needs to be paid

And all I have left

Is bottom of the pocket-book change?

How I can go through and still look serene

As the water in a mountain lake?

Here's how I do it:

I don't get in bed with the devil

Bemoaning every trial and tribulation,

I look to God and Consider every day a revelation.

Trust me on this,

You can get through

Anything, if you pray

Just pray your way through.

You have no time for stressing

When you're counting all your blessings.

A Tribute to a Friend

September 19, 2017 was one of the saddest days of my life. I attended the funeral of my College Roommate and friend, **JoAnn Eason Williams**. Those of you who have read my book, **Promise of Friendship**, know what a premium I place on friendship. Anyone I honor with the title of "friend" has an extraordinary place in my heart.

I know that most people in my age group (50 years out of high school) have suffered a heart-rendering loss of a loved one. So, I will not claim that my loss is more significant than what others have gone through. I only know that losing my best friend hurts beyond my power to express in words. I also know that it hurts more since the loss was unexpected. I should have guessed that her illness was more severe than she let on. I should have known that there had to be a serious reason why the JoAnn that I knew was no longer driving. But she said that she was home now and that her family and friends were taking good care of her, making sure that she had meals and got to all her appointments. So, I only fussed a little bit about her not having someone let me know that she had been in the hospital then I let the issue drop.

I knew that, even though I was six months older than her, JoAnn had appointed herself my big sister. After all, she pledged Alpha Kappa Alpha and went over before I did, and she was my Dean of Pledgees when I went over. In a sisterly way, she taught me all the things a girl who had grown up in a Pentecostal Holiness Church had, according to JoAnn, missed out on. She demanded that I learn how to "coordinate" everything- pocketbook with shoes, dress with earrings, and stockings with a dress.

She taught me to be proud of my roots. While other classmates were claiming to be from the closest large city (Students from Oxford claimed to be from Raleigh, those from Winsor claimed Elizabeth City or Greenville, etc.), JoAnn proudly proclaimed that she was from Sunbury, North Carolina. When we graduated from college in 1970, Dean Keys, who was over Shaw University's Centennial Scholars Program, recommended her for a teaching job at a private school in Michigan. When they offered her the job, she turned them down because she only wanted to teach in her hometown.

JoAnn was a true Southern Belle. She insisted that we put on make-up, girdles, and dress-up for our 7:30 a.m. American Literature Class with Dr. Altman, even though it was clear after the first day that no one else bothered to so much as wash their face. She would not let me rest until I'd hemmed all except one of my dresses, which were mid-calf length to the proper late 1960's length - mini skirt length (We left one dress long so that I had something to wear to church when I went home). She made it impossible for me to sleep in later than 5:30 a.m. She had one of those old fashion alarm clocks that could wake someone from a coma. She said that we had to get up that early so that we had time to dress appropriately to go to breakfast before class. She said that breakfast was brain fuel.

JoAnn took friendship to the next level. She prodded me to do my best. She understood that I was shy rather than standoffish. So, she maneuvered me into situations that I would never have attempted on my own. We went across town to N.C. State University to see the movie, *Putney Swope*. We went to eat at Clyde's Barbecue and sat in the section designated for Whites Only. She taught me to be aware of what was going on around me in every situation. When my youngest sister needed a navy-blue suit and gold blouse to be in Dudley High School's Homecoming Court, she went with me Downtown to Lerner's. She paid for the outfit with her charge card. Then, she asked the saleslady for a pair of scissors and cut the charge card-up in the woman's face. Then she said, pointing as she spoke, "You know that brown leather jacket that was on that rack over there and that red outfit that was over there. Those white girls who were in here with us walked out with all that while you were so busy watching us. My mother will be reporting you to the Regional Office." I had been so focused on getting that outfit to my sister that I hadn't noticed anything. If that woman had noticed those items missing after we left, JoAnn and I would have been the ones she accused of shoplifting. Our careers as teachers and upstanding citizens would have been over before they began.

JoAnn would help anyone who needed her help, but she refused to allow anyone to take advantage of her or take her for granted. I learned that lesson the hard way. She could type fast, and I still cannot type very well. She would type my papers for me, but only if I had the assignment neatly handwritten a couple of days before it was due. One time, I didn't have my assignment ready to type until the night before it was due. She refused to type it. She went to bed at her regular bedtime, 10:00 p.m. She laid there all-night tossing and turning, while I struggled to type three pages. The next morning, she got up, looked at me with red eyes swollen from lack of sleep, and said, "Don't ever put me through a night like that again. You can do better." I made sure that I did better from then on.

The last thing that JoAnn taught me was not to put off spending time with someone you love. We spoke on the phone regularly-each time for hours. We kept planning to spend a long weekend or full week together for the last four years, but we kept putting it off. I had not seen her in person since she and Otis came to Greensboro for a convention when she was on the Gates County Board of Health. Dying JoAnn taught me to seize every opportunity to share time with a special friend or love one because you never know when those opportunities will end.

I want the family (Vivian Knight and Tonya Knight), friends, Classmates, Church members at St. John AME Zion Church in Sunbury, and co-workers of JoAnn Celestine Eason Williams, to know that I envy you the time that you had with her. Still, I will always cherish the 49 years 11 months and 12 days that she was my best friend.

For Paige

Baby Girl

I always wanted

At least 10 grandchildren

But God saw fit

To give me only one

Granddaughter.

One Paige

Is enough

To tell my story

Of love and faith.

One Paige

Is smart enough

Caring enough

Hard working enough

To be the best.

One Paige is enough to make me proud.

Go on

Grandma's girl

And become all God made you to be.

For SirMason

You are All that

And then some!

Never allow others

To tell you how far

you can go.

Or set limits on your

accomplishments.

You know what is in you.

Because I told you so.

You are smart.

You are capable.

You are strong.

I am depending

on you

To carry the banner that says,

"I am a proud Black Man."

Remember Me

If I ever loved, you
I still do.
If I ever stood with you
I'm still there.
If I ever made you laugh
Smile now
When you think of me.
If I ever prayed for you
He is still listening.
If I ever said you can do it,
You still can.
If I ever held you close
Remember those hugs and kisses
When I'm gone.

Footwear

I started my walk in cotton socks
With lace around the edges
White starched pinafores
Little aprons in the best little girl style
To Sunday school we walked a good three miles.
Then bobby socks
Carried me well into my teens
To WPWW and lectures
From Sister King

In stockings with seams
I strutted into womanhood.
I never learned how to keep
Seams straight on bow legs,
Or how to keep from getting runs
On benches made of wood.
Only the old mothers ever mastered
How to keep them from rolling
Down to their ankles when they shouted.
Now I am walking in pantie hose
That i suppose
Were sent directly from heaven
God knew how He'd made us-
Little, medium, big and small
And that one size could never fit all.

www.ingramcontent.com/pod-product-compliance
Lightning Source LLC
Chambersburg PA
CBHW070858050426
42453CB00012B/2261